Cloud Computing for Nonprofits

Patrick Callihan

Cloud Computing for Nonprofits

Published by Tech Impact

Email: patrick@techimpact.org

Phone: (215) 557-1559

URL: http://www.techimpact.org

Cover by: Caroline Chen, Chengraphix.com

ISBN 978-1-304-34993-4

DEDICATION

To those people who get up every morning with the spirit and drive to
help somebody else and to make our world a better place,
especially the dedicated team and board of directors at Tech Impact.

ACKNOWLEDGMENTS

I am grateful to my father who bought me my first computer and put the power of technology in my hands. I am also thankful to my wife and family for their unending support.

I sincerely appreciate all of those who have taught me along the way, there are many. I will try to pass it on.

Foreword

"If GM had kept up with technology like the computer industry has, we would all be driving $25 cars that get 1,000 MPG."

-Bill Gates

Technology changes rapidly. It is one of the things that attracted me to it, and has kept me engaged, in a twenty-five year career that always included some aspect of technology. I thrive on change; technology is perfect for me.

Over the span of my career, I have witnessed trends. The trend right now is clearly a path to cloud computing. There are those who say we are just returning to a model that was in place before: a centralized computing model. On the surface, that may seem true. But many things have changed since then. We now have significantly more bandwidth, we have virtualization, and we have automation. I will explain those in this book, but it is important to realize that this trend it is different.

Much more exciting to me than cloud computing is the impact on the nonprofits I care about—those that are doing good work every day to care for things that are vulnerable: our children, the elderly, abandoned pets, and the environment, among others. It is exciting to me because nonprofits now have access to much of the infrastructure and tools that were reserved for the big corporations with deep pockets. Just a few years ago, nonprofits could never have afforded the same technology luxuries as corporations. That has changed. Much of the same software that is used by Fortune 500 companies is now readily available to nonprofits. And, in many cases, it is donated. That is exciting.

This book is not meant to be a comprehensive technology manual. It is meant to explain to nonprofit leaders, in plain English, what is important about technology for their mission and how to obtain that technology.

My hope is that nonprofit leaders will not spend their valuable time thinking about technology and instead will focus on what's most important: advancing their missions. Nonprofits deserve the same technology as larger corporations—technology that works so well it is seamless.

I am glad that technology continues to improve and advance; it means nonprofit operations can become more efficient while spending less. These two things translate into more people served through our missions.

Contents

Part I - The Fundamentals

Chapter 1: What is cloud computing and why should I care?

I am going to answer those two questions in reverse order.

You should care because if you are a nonprofit leader, it will help you and your staff be more effective and efficient in delivering your mission. You should care because computing in general is trending to cloud computing and you have a responsibility to keep up with the advancement of technology for the sake of your organization.

A few years ago, I was at a technology conference hosted by Gartner, computer industry analysts. The speaker painted this picture:

You are an entrepreneur with a great idea for a new piece of software and you give your pitch to a group of investors. They love your idea and then ask you about packaging and distribution. You answer by explaining you will burn the software to CDs, put them in a nicely packaged box, and distribute them to Best Buy so they can be sold to millions of people all across the country. The investors thank you for your time and send you packing back to Starbucks to reconsider your distribution plans.

Have you been to a Best Buy lately? Not only are the music aisles gone, but so are the software aisles. Recently, software companies moved to web-based distribution, just like music sales. You can go to their websites and download whatever software you need, without getting in your car. They cut out the middle man.

Today, most software companies have figured out a new sales model: recurring revenue. This was largely driven by company valuations. If you want to start a company, build it, and eventually sell it, you will get the highest valuation if you have built recurring revenues. It is much easier to acquire a client and keep them than to find new clients each month. This model was enabled by cloud computing.

Think about the big giants. Microsoft's model was to develop software, like Windows, and then, every few years, sell it to you again, as an upgrade. In fact, they often end support of a product after a new version is released. Think of the difficulty in that model. Every few years, they would need to meet with their clients and convince them that they needed to upgrade their software. Microsoft has a lot of customers, which takes a lot of salespeople and salespeople are expensive. But in their current business model, they do not sell software anymore; they lease it. You will never upgrade; you will *be* upgraded.

Cloud computing has enabled an entirely new, highly profitable business model that is also very effective. End users will no longer need to think about the upgrade process; it will just happen. There are other benefits: it scales, it is predictable, and it is easily accessible.

As a nonprofit leader, this is important. It is important because you are going to budget for technology differently than you have before. You should be including a line item in your budget for software—not software *purchases*, but software *leasing*. The good news is that much of this software, because you are a nonprofit, is donated. Not only is Microsoft very smart at developing software and new business models, but they are incredibly generous.

But you really need to care because cloud computing is the future. It is here. I do not know of a single software developer that is not planning to distribute their software product on the cloud. You need to care because you will eventually have no other choice. If you take steps now to embrace this new model, you will bring efficiencies and cost savings to your organization. You will reduce the dependency on technology grants and general operating dollars, and I am going to show you how.

Now, for the first question, what is the cloud? That is going to be a little more difficult to answer.

Let's start here: Where did the term *cloud* come from?

That part is simple. Have you ever seen a network diagram? I hope the answer is no. If it is yes, this book may not be for you. Either way, the network diagram that follows uses a number of symbols to depict what is inside a computer network—servers, computers, etc. Notice that when something goes to the internet, it is depicted by a cloud. That is where the term comes from—cloud represents the internet.

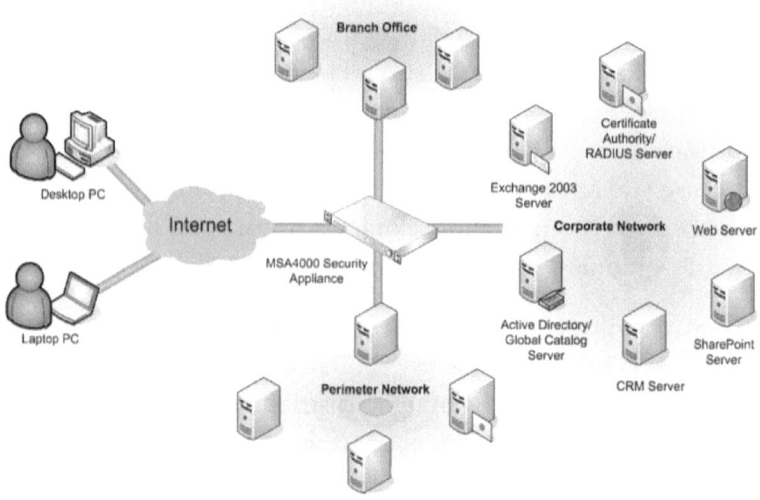

Let me stop here and give the definition of **cloud computing**:

A general term for anything that involves delivering

hosted <u>services</u> over the internet.

While many commercials on television and the radio would have you believe that cloud computing will make you a better spouse, improve your love life, and make you coffee in the morning, the truth is it is nothing more than a service delivered over the internet.

Most of us use cloud computing every single day. If you have a Facebook account or do your banking online, you are using cloud computing. These are services that are delivered over the internet. There is nothing for us to download; we simply go on to the internet and use the service.

There are, however, different types of services that can be delivered through cloud computing. It is important to break it down just a little further. You may have seen these acronyms- SaaS, IaaS, and PaaS. There are more "aaS'es" out there, but these are the big three. They stand for Software as a Service (SaaS), Infrastructure as a Service (IaaS), and Platform as a Service (PaaS).

Software as a Service

The most important of the three to understand is SaaS. It is also the most common in our industry. Facebook is a great example of Software as a Service. Not that long ago, if you wanted to use a service like Facebook to stay in touch with your friends and family (and let them know about all the cool stuff you do) you may have needed to download some piece of software to your computer that would have come from Best Buy or, eventually, from a web download. Today, that software does not need to be on your computer. It does not require your operating system. All you need to do is go to the internet and type www.facebook.com. All of the software that you are using resides on their servers and computers and not yours.

That software delivery brings several advantages. If I get a new computer, I do not need to reload that software. If I am using someone else's computer, I can simply navigate to the internet. Nothing is saved or stored on the computer. It is also really fast and easy to use that service. And when Facebook upgrades its software and makes changes, I do not need to download the changes or upgrade my software. I simply navigate to the account and notice the changes that have been made.

Now, Facebook is more consumer facing, but there are many examples of common nonprofit software that many of us use every day. The most common I can think of is email. All of us use email to communicate with our donors, volunteers, fellow associates, and clients. The easiest example of SaaS based email is Gmail. If you have ever used Gmail, you have used a software as a service email system. You did not need to download a program to open an account or to start sending messages.

Some examples of software as a service include LinkedIn, Twitter, Skype, Office365, and Drop Box, to name just a few.

Platform as a Service

PaaS, or platform as a service, is a little different. This is primarily for developers. If you want to develop software, there are certain things you usually need. First, you need development software like .Net, Java, or Visual Basic. Then, you need to load that software onto a machine or server (definitely a server if you have more than one developer). Then you may want a second server with a second set of software licenses so that you can test. Finally, you would need a server to run the production version. You can see, this starts to get more complicated and expensive. Now, some companies have developed these software platforms as a service. One of the most widely used is the Salesforce.com platform, named Force.com.

Developers on the Force.com platform can develop software without downloading it to their local computer network. They can build and deploy applications on the platform, even sell and distribute them, without owning anything. This is a game changer for developers. This enables many entrepreneurs to build and market their own applications in a fraction of the time and with a fraction of the investment. This is part of what is enabling the many apps on the Apple platform that we now take for granted in our everyday lives.

Infrastructure as a Service

Finally, there is IaaS, or Infrastructure as a Service. The easiest way to think of infrastructure is as the plumbing of computing. This is the server, the storage device, or the networking equipment. It is probably the equipment that is stuffed into a closet or back room somewhere in your facility. Instead of owning and operating this equipment, you can now lease it over the web. There are a number of advantages to leasing infrastructure. The first is that you own nothing. Owning a server is expensive. There is the cost of purchasing the server. Then there is the ongoing maintenance of the server, like adding software patches when they are periodically released. There is also risk because a server is a piece of equipment that has moving parts that can and eventually will break. If you have ever experienced a failed disk drive in your server, you know what I mean. It can be devastating for an organization. If that server runs your email system, you can be without email until it is repaired. Repairs can take days and even weeks in some cases. If your server is not properly backed up, you will have a very difficult time recovering your data. Regardless, eventually your server will need to be replaced.

When it is, there will be the cost of a new server, the cost to configure and install the server, and the cost to migrate your data from your old server to the new one. Servers are expensive. When you lease infrastructure, you are only paying for the computing power that you need. And, generally someone else is responsible for maintaining the physical layer and the operating system. It is not necessarily inexpensive, although prices are coming down, but it is predictable. More or less, I find that the costs of leasing infrastructure are on the surface a little more expensive, but there are many soft costs to consider as well, including, floor space, electricity, and staff time. All in all, I think IaaS is worth considering if you must run your own servers.

We will explore this topic further in later chapters.

Generally speaking, I encourage the nonprofits I work with to move toward cloud computing as much as they are able. Because that is the trend in computing, I believe all organizations will eventually end up on 100% cloud computing platforms. I think it is wise to embrace this trend early and start to prepare the nonprofit to move with the trend. For most organizations, especially those that have operating budgets under one million dollars, it makes a great deal of sense. It makes sense economically, and it makes sense operationally. There is less to own and maintain, and it often provides a better disaster recovery and

For most organizations, especially those that have operating budgets under one million dollars, it makes a great deal of sense. It makes sense economically, and it makes sense operationally.

business continuity plan than what you currently have in place.

Chapter 2: What makes the cloud the cloud?

Now we know that the cloud is a service that is delivered over the internet. But what makes that possible?

There are several contributing factors that have enabled cloud computing. They have all come together at the right time, a perfect storm, so to speak, to drive the cloud revolution. I am going to break them down for you here.

The first is bandwidth. Bandwidth is simply the number of bits of information that travel through a communication path. It is how we transfer data, or information, from one place to another over the web and the speed in which we are able to do so.

In the early days of the internet, most of us had dial up capability. The phrase "You've Got Mail" may come to mind when you heard your modem connect to the email service. The amount of bandwidth on a dial up connection is 56kbps. That means it could transfer 56,000 kilobytes of information in a second. A kilobyte is 1024 bytes of information and a byte is 8 bits. A bit is a binary value, either a 0 or a 1. So that was a lot of 0s and 1s (almost a half-million) that it could transfer in a second. The computer on the other end of the communication line translated the 0s and 1s into valid information. So it took lot of bits and bytes to make logical information, like an email, appear.

A rate of 56 thousand bits per second travelling from one computer to another over a communication line seemed like a great service. Fast forward to today. The basic offering from your local cable company probably offers service of about 5Mbs, or five million megabytes, per second. A megabyte is 1,024 kilobytes of information. In short, a 5Mbs connection sends 45 million bits of information per second. That is a huge improvement. This means, effectively, that much more data can transfer between computers in the same time. Speeds of 50 megabytes per second can be purchased for around $100 a month.

Bandwidth is a game changer; it fuels massive amounts of information being exchanged over communication lines. (The internet).

While the cost of bandwidth has remained somewhat constant over the years, the amount of bandwidth for the dollar has increased substantially. Keep in mind that much of this explosion of bandwidth has happened in just the last decade or so. Bandwidth is a game changer; it fuels massive amounts of information being exchanged over communication lines. This reduces the need for your local computer to house software. In cloud computing, you simply access the software over the internet.

Bandwidth alone is not the only thing fueling the adoption of cloud computing. Virtualization is playing a major role as well.

One of the most recent inventions in computing software is virtualization. Virtualization software allows computer users to create virtual instances of the computer. In other words, they can break up the physical resources into virtual resources. A typical computer is made up of various physical components: a hard disc, a memory chip, a micro processer, and a networking card. Virtualization software allows those components to be parsed. So instead of a computer that has 250 gigabytes of storage on a disc drive, perhaps you could have two virtual storage discs of 125 gigabytes each. I do not want to get into a great deal of detail because this book is really meant to educate readers about cloud computing and not be a technical manual. The important concept here is that virtualization software allows a user to take a physical piece of hardware and break it into one or many virtual pieces of hardware.

There are a few advantages to virtualization architecture. The first is efficiency. Because computer resource (disc drives, processer chips, etc.) costs continue to fall, many of the machines that are available for purchase have much more disc space and memory than we may need. This is especially true of servers. A small nonprofit that operates its own server may only be using 10-15% of the capacity of that server. The same goes for businesses, especially because servers are only meant to have one operating system and usually one application. So even large businesses that have servers only use a small amount of the capacity of those servers. This is inefficient. However, when virtualized into numerous servers, a physical server can start to reach the physical capacity of the hardware.

Since there may be four virtual servers on one physical server, the amount of hardware resources used are increased exponentially.

Another advantage is that virtual servers are developed as a file. This means that if you need to move a virtual server from one physical machine to another, then you only need move a file—much like a file on your documents folder or a file of music. The reason this is an advantage is that moving a file is much easier, and faster, than rebuilding a server. It also means that the information can be replicated easily to another location. This is particularly important for disaster recovery and business continuity. Since files may be copied and stored on multiple virtual, or physical, machines it allows for your data to be easily replicated and kept safe. Good cloud computing vendors keep multiple copies of your data and store them on computers that are geographically dispersed more than 1,000 miles apart to account for a possible disaster that strike.

This picture, published by VMWare, does a good job at depicting what a virtual server looks like:

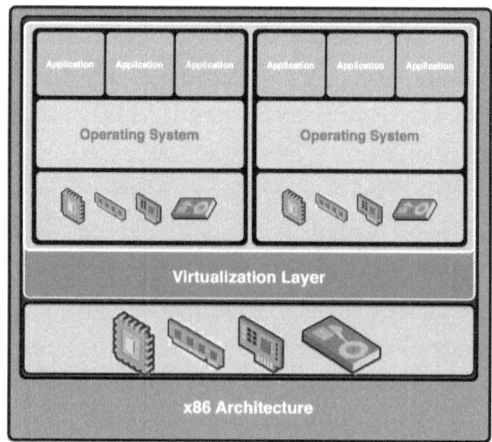

The illustration demonstrates two virtual servers that are part of a single physical server. Here you can see two different operating systems and six applications housed on the two virtual servers.

Other things that are making the cloud possible include Automated Data Center software and Commodity Hardware.

Most of us have probably toured a data center. It may have been a cold room on raised flooring that had rows of computers and blinking lights. Data centers have become more efficient over the years and have required fewer resources to run them. There has been a great deal of software developed that help to run those operations. This is especially important when it comes to virtualization. Since all servers eventually stop working, it is important that data center operators know when that happens so they can transfer all of the applications and data from the failed machine to another machine. Today, some software can recognize when a failure is taking place and automatically move the virtual files from one physical machine to another without human intervention. That software can also set up routine functions, like operating system updates or file copies, automatically. The point is that automated software helps reduce the cost of running and maintaining those computers. These are the same computers that are used for cloud computing, so it makes the operation more efficient, which is important in lowering the cost of cloud computing. Remember that when you lease software over the internet, you are not only paying for the software, but you are paying for the hosting of where your data and that application are stored. The more efficient those operations are, the more competitive the pricing for cloud computing becomes.

The same goes for commodity hardware. The hardware today that runs in a data center is becoming more and more standardized and may be stripped down. It may not have the cover that you are accustomed to seeing on a server, it may not have as many peripherals, and it may have only the most basic of components. This is because servers are not built to look nice; they are built to perform. They may be part of a massive cluster of servers that operate a cloud computing operation. This also helps drive down cost and increase efficiency.

This is a good time to show you the cloud. I hope that by now you have learned that the cloud is not a single thing but a type of computing. There is not one cloud, but many. Since cloud computing is a service delivered over the internet, the cloud you are accessing is at the other end of that communication line. The cloud may be Amazon, Microsoft, Salesforce.com, or something else. It is wherever you are procuring those services.

Here is a picture of the Microsoft data center in Chicago:

You will notice what looks like shipping containers. They are in fact shipping containers. Inside the containers are clusters of commodity servers. The servers have been networked together to the point that all an operator needs to do is to connect these containers to a power source and turn them on. The software inside is highly automated. These server clusters can now manage data for thousands of customers. Here is what they look like on the inside:

Because companies like Microsoft have so much experience with servers, they can predict failure rates on these machines. They know about how many will fail and over what time period. When it is no longer efficient to operate one of these containers because a number of the servers inside have failed, then can decommission the container and send it back to their supplier to be outfit with a new cluster of servers. This is how commoditized the server farms have become.

Microsoft operates numerous data centers all over the world. When you are on the Microsoft Cloud, your data is stored in at least two of these centers at all times so that it can be easily recovered if there is a hardware failure that impacted your data. This is reassuring to me since, as a nonprofit, I could never afford this type of architecture in my own operation.

What really enables cloud computing are virtualization, commodity hardware, automated data center software, and bandwidth. These are things that were not present when centralized computing was popular in the late 1980s. This is what makes cloud computing so much different today. It is also what makes it an incredibly efficient and secure model. This is why we are moving toward cloud computing.

Chapter 3: Characteristics of Cloud Computing

There are a number of characteristics that distinguish cloud computing from client server-based technology. Think of cloud computing as a utility. It is fairly easy to turn on and fairly easy to turn off. Once you turn it on, you do not have to think about it much, beyond paying the monthly invoice. It is scalable and somehow metered.

"Just like water from the tap in your kitchen, cloud computing services can be turned on or off quickly as needed. Like at the water company, there is a team of dedicated professionals making sure the service provided is safe, secure and available on a 24/7 basis. When the tap isn't on, not only are you saving water, but you aren't paying for resources you don't currently need."

- Vivek Kundra, CIO in Obama administration

The characteristics are important to remember because many IT providers will try to sell you cloud solutions. But if they do not have these characteristics, and a few more, they are not cloud solutions.

Marc Benioff, founder of Salesforce.com, said, "If you are in a private cloud, you are not in a cloud." There are IT vendors that will talk about "Private Cloud." This means it is exclusively your cloud and your applications are not multi-tenanted. But the whole point of cloud computing is to multi-tenant the applications to gain efficiency. I would call this type of cloud a co-location, which simply means moving your servers out of your facility to a data center. You may be outsourcing the management of those servers, but they are *your* servers. When they fail, you will need to replace them. That is not cloud computing.

To be considered *cloud*, your applications must be metered. In other words, you only pay for what you use. If you are using applications, you pay for the number of users. If you are using infrastructure, you usually pay for the computing cycles. Either way, your invoice changes based on your usage. And your usage is scalable. If you add another staff member and need a new email box set up, you just provision it and expect your bill to increase by one license. Likewise, when someone leaves your organization, you downsize the number of mailboxes and expect your invoice to reflect the lower amount next month.

The cloud is generally self-provisioning. If I want to set up a new email address for myself, I can go online to Google and probably have a new email account established in a few minutes. I do not need anyone's help. I do not need to hire an IT company or even contact Google. I am able to self-provision the account. I can also de-provision the account.

The cloud is available on demand. Not only am I able to provision and de-provision an account online, I am able to access that account at any time. It is available on demand. More likely, I am probably able to access that application or service from any location. This is what is meant by "anytime, anywhere." (And is usually followed by "from any device.") True cloud computing applications do not care where you are, what time it is, or what browser you are using. They are truly on demand.

Finally, cloud computing is managed. You never should have to worry about the operating system upgrade, server failure, or rebooting the service. It should be automatic. There is a team of people at the cloud provider that works hard to

> **Finally, cloud computing is managed. You never should have to worry about the operating system upgrade, server failure, or rebooting the service. It should be automatic.**

ensure you do not need to worry about how you are getting those services; you only need to worry about how best to use those services.

Probably the most important thing when you are using cloud computing services is knowing your cloud provider. You want to know who is behind that infrastructure and who is behind that application. You will want to read your vendor's service level agreements, what the likelihood of their existence is in the near future, how they are managing your data, and how to get your data back if you should need or want it back. You can evaluate the services based on these characteristics.

Chapter 4: A Few Words about Data Security

TechSoup, a nonprofit that provides access to discounted software, recently surveyed over 10,000 nonprofit employees about cloud computing. They asked a number of questions about adoption of cloud computing. Forty-five percent of those surveyed cited data security as a concern and barrier for adopting cloud computing; 54% said the opposite—that improved data security is the reason they are using or considering cloud computing solutions. I suppose 1% decided not to answer the question.

Whenever I speak about cloud computing, the issue of security always comes up. And it should. Data security is a big deal. Every day on the internet there are millions of cyber-attacks. An article I read recently in the *New York Times*

The University of Wisconsin estimates they receive between 90,000 and 100,000 attempts per day that originate from China that are attempting to penetrate their system.

outlined some of the challenges that universities are facing with cyber-attacks. The University of Wisconsin estimates that they receive between 90,000 and 100,000 attempts per day that originate from China that are attempting to penetrate their system.

Some of today's headlines have a lot to say about data security. As I am writing this, there is a former NSA hacker who is held up in Russia because he disclosed information to China about how the United States spies on other countries' data. Of course the NSA itself has been hacked. Major corporations have been hacked, including Sony, Citigroup, and Google, to name a few. You may be thinking, "Not us. We are a small nonprofit. Why would anyone want to hack our network?" Symantec, a leading software company that provides security software, recently reported that almost one third of all cyber-attacks are against small businesses.

One of the main differences between large enterprises and small businesses is that as a small business you may not even realize you have been hacked. Are you checking the server logs? Do you have a firewall that is maintained and updated with the latest patches? Do you have strict policies about how employees share and store information? Are any of your employees using outside storage like Dropbox? You can begin to see some of the complexities in managing and monitoring data security policies.

This is one of the reasons I favor outsourcing my data to a cloud computing provider. Even as the director of an IT company, one of my biggest concerns is data security, and I know we are not equipped to manage and maintain all of our data in the safest way possible. I worry about data leaks and undetected hacking on our networks. I simply cannot afford to hire a data security expert on my staff, as they command six figure salaries. To me, working with a company that has expertise in managing security is a better option. I am among the 54% in the TechSoup survey. One of the reasons my organization has embraced cloud computing is data security.

This goes back to knowing the cloud provider that is managing your data. I use larger providers like Microsoft, Salesforce.com, and NetSuite. I know these companies employ security professionals—probably thousands of them. Their businesses depend on security. It is not to say that they cannot be breached, of course they can. But if they are breached, they are more likely to know it and more likely to mitigate the threat much faster than I could. This does not eliminate the threat, but it does reduce it. I have been briefed on some of the extreme measures that Microsoft takes to ensure data security. They are far more advanced than anything my nonprofit is capable of doing to mitigate threats.

As a nonprofit, I would encourage you to look at your data and computing practices. What measures are you taking to ensure the security of your data? What data are you managing? Do you take credit cards? Do you have names and addresses of your donors? Do you store social security numbers of your employees? How about for your clients? It is wise to do a complete assessment of your data and know where it is stored, who has access, and how it is backed up.

There is no silver bullet for this one. If you think you have great security practices in place, hire an ethical hacker to try to hack your network or website. He or she will give you a report that tells if the hackers were able to get into your system, how they got in, and what measures you can take to prevent an attack. It is difficult because there are new types of attacks every day and there are new security vulnerabilities found in software every day. But being aware of any vulnerabilities you may have is the first step toward achieving a safe computing environment.

If you decide to outsource data management, know about the security practices of your provider. What measures do they have in place for security? Make sure you trust the organizations that you are working with. I have found that there are major differences between a local cloud provider and a company like Microsoft. I am not saying that smaller companies are not competent— many are very competent. But I tend to favor larger companies that have more resources, or companies that specialize in cloud computing because they understand the vulnerabilities and take measures to prevent being infiltrated.

Chapter 5: Risks and Benefits of Cloud Computing

As with most things in life, there are risks and there are benefits. The hope is that the benefits outweigh the risks and that there are ways to mitigate risks. In some cases, as I will point out, a risk can actually become a benefit.

The previous chapter explored one of the risks of cloud computing: data security. If you skipped that section, give it a read. It is not technical and it may help you to understand the risks in data security. If you are contemplating a move to cloud computing, make sure you know your vendor. This is a common theme throughout this book, but cannot be overstated.

One of the greatest risks to cloud computing is loss of connectivity. Obviously, if you are relying on services that are delivered over the internet, and you lose your internet connection, you will not be able to get to your services. What causes internet outages? Lots of things. It could be something as simple as a failed piece of hardware, like a router. It could be that your provider lost its connection. It could be that a construction crew cut a fiber by mistake. Of course, other causes, like flooding and fire, can play a role in the ability to receive an internet connection at your office. It happens, connections go down. Hopefully it does not happen often, but it can be a risk.

Another risk is loss of data. Yes, cloud computing providers have lost data. Some years ago, one of the leading cloud backup providers lost the data of over 7,000 customers. That is a big deal. It could have been prevented. One of the questions you want to ask your cloud provider is how data is stored and whether they maintain a redundant copy, and, if so, where. Data centers come in various classifications. Tier one data centers, for instance, only have a single non-redundant distribution path and have non-redundant capacity components. This means that if their internet provider goes down, they go down. By contrast, a tier four data center not only has redundant carriers, but they also have redundant power supplies and a backup diesel generator. Tier four data centers are equipped to be operational during the worst of times. This does make them more expensive, but if you have a critical business operation, it may be worth the cost. Some providers maintain a single copy of your data. Others maintain redundant copies of your data and may store the additional copy in a data center that is more than 1,000 miles apart from the original data center. This is done in case of a regional disaster, like a hurricane or major earthquake. Again, it will be more expensive, but it may be worth it for your data. What is important to understand is what risks you are taking on when you sign the contract.

Another risk is understanding the viability of the service provider. What do you know about them? Are they profitable or are they in danger of going out of business? Who are their investors? Are they growing? I do not think you need to run a complete financial evaluation on each vendor, but you should know something about them. A few minutes of research on the web will probably tell you plenty. Do they have any pending litigations? Do clients give their solutions good reviews? You may want to run a background check of sorts to make sure that the company you are going to work with is viable and are experts in their field. Every provider should be able to give you a list of the Service Level Agreements that they provide. Most will give you some sort of guarantee of 99.9% to 99.99999% uptime for their applications and systems.

If you were to run a quick scan on the internet, I am sure you could come up with other threats. Most of the big ones surround data security. The single most important piece of advice I can give you when considering cloud computing providers is to know your provider.

I mentioned earlier that one of the risks -connectivity- could actually be a benefit. At least that is how I see it. If I am working in the office and lose connectivity to the internet, I can no longer access my cloud-based services. And, as I mentioned, there are a number of things that can cause a loss of connectivity, including bad hardware or a cut line. In some cases, like fire and flooding, I could be offline for days or weeks. Normally that would be devastating to an organization that relies on computers to communicate with clients, with each other, partners, etc. However, if you are leveraging cloud computing and you lose a connection, you have the ability to relocate and find another connection.

Let me articulate this a little further. During the recent devastating hurricane on the east coast, Hurricane Sandy, we worked with several organizations that had their offices flooded. They were relying on servers. Their servers were no longer working because they were under water. Electricity had been cut off to their buildings. They were struggling to get operational again. They had to look for alternative communication methods. Had they been using an online email system that relied on the cloud, they could have accessed their services from home or from their local Starbucks. Since cloud technology only relies on an internet connection, they could essentially access their applications from anywhere they could find that had an internet connection. So, yes, there is a risk of losing connectivity. But when you do, at least you can go someplace else that has connectivity. If you lose power in your office and your server is at your office, you are crippled until that service is restored. This is an advantage I see to cloud computing.

There are other pluses. With cloud computing there is nothing to own. You do not purchase the software, you rent it. If you are unhappy with the program, you rent another one. Yes, you will have to pay for the data migration, but at least you can move without making a significant investment. This also gives you the ability to rent one license of a particular software program. You can trial the software before moving all of your users to something new. Along the same lines, the cloud generally

I can be halfway around the world without my computer, and if I can get access to a device and the internet … I can access all of my applications and data- my email, my accounting reports, my customer data…. All of this without being in my office and without having my computer. That is powerful.

has a rapid deployment model. It is fast to procure a new software title and generally even faster to set up a new user. You can scale quickly.

You may have also heard the words "anytime, anywhere." This is a cloud characteristic and benefit.

One of the biggest advantages of cloud computing is the ability to reduce expenses on capital and, in particular, on infrastructure. In the next chapter, I will discuss budgeting. But it is worth exploring the idea behind reduced infrastructure. The computers that we have been purchasing and supplying to our employees have stayed fairly relative in price, but much higher in performance. It is now hard to find a desktop or laptop that does not have at least a 250 GB hard drive— most probably have 500 GB or even 1TB. Does anyone really store this much stuff on their work machines? If they do, is it work- related or is it their iTunes collection?

Computers are constantly becoming more powerful; that is Moore's law. But with cloud computing, we are offloading the processing and storage, essentially the computing, to a server someplace else: the cloud. If most of the storage and processing are being delivered as a service, then we do not need as powerful machines. You may have heard of thin clients, netbooks, Chromebooks, and zero clients. These are the newer machines that have less computing power. They are designed for cloud computing. In some cases, they have a very small operating system, which allows the machines to boot up very quickly, some in just a few seconds. From there, they rely on the internet for most of the services.

Let's take a look at Chromebook, a Google product. The idea behind Chromebook is that it is a relatively inexpensive internet appliance. It looks like a laptop. It has a keyboard and screen. But it has a very small software footprint—so small that the machine can boot up in less than 10 seconds. That is really fast. It only has 16 GB of storage, a far cry from the 250 GB that most laptops have as a minimum. And, the storage is usually solid state. This means it has no moving parts, like a spinning disk, so it should last longer and require fewer repairs. The price of this machine starts at $199. That is considerably less than a laptop. It is at least half the price and probably closer to 80% less than the price of most machines that I see purchased by nonprofits. Chromebook is designed to work well with Google products like Gmail and Google Drive. Netbooks are exactly the same, only they are not Google centric. The price tag is the same, starting at under $200.

Thin clients and zero clients are more like desktop computers. They are small boxes that sit on the desk and connect to a monitor, keyboard, and mouse. Like netbooks, they have a very small software/operating system. They are designed to boot up quickly and access the internet. They usually cost around $250, again considerably less than the $800-$1,000 that I see most nonprofits spend on desktop computers for their employees.

This is the future of computing. If we receive all of our services over the internet, and we are able to access those services with less powerful— and less costly— appliances, then we will not need a server. In our office, we have eliminated the Exchange email server, shared file server, and application server. We have all of those services on the cloud. If you think laptops and desktop computers are expensive, then you may want to look at what you spent on the last server you purchased.

I expect that in the not-too-distant future, we will not buy laptops and desktops. They will become obsolete. For the first time in the history of microcomputers, we experienced a global decline in the last quarter of the number of computers ordered and shipped. This is only the beginning. I like to draw the analogy between computers and cameras. When the digital camera was first introduced it was very expensive. Over time, the price dropped to a point where most people could afford a $100-$200 camera. Every year, the technology improved, and we got a few more megapixels of resolution for the dollar. If we owned one of these and it broke, it was unlikely that we would get it fixed. In most cases, it would cost us more to repair the camera than to buy a new one. And besides, if it had been a couple of years since purchasing one, the technology would have improved significantly for about the same price tag. I believe computers are headed in the same direction.

How much do you pay for computer support? I would guess around $75-$125 an hour. That is generally the market. So if you have a thin client that you purchased for $250 and it breaks, would you have it repaired? It may cost you the time of the technician's travel, plus repair time. It can easily reach the $200 level. It may not be worth it, especially if you pay that only to find out that it cannot be repaired. Or would you simply purchase a new one at $250 with the latest technology? I know how I would answer that question. Before long, this is how computing will work for most of us. This is an advantage of cloud computing: the need for less powerful and less costly machines. But there is also the convenience factor.

If you have ever traveled with a laptop, you know how cumbersome that can be. With cloud technology, you can access your applications from any device that has a web browser and an internet connection. That means that you can pull out your smartphone or tablet computer and access the exact same information. That makes traveling much more pleasant. And it makes it easier to access information when you are at home, as well. For nonprofits that have field workers or a geographically dispersed workforce, cloud computing makes a great deal of sense.

While there are some risks associated with cloud computing, these risks will only continue to decline over time, especially as the market consolidates. The benefits, on the other hand, are numerous. Regardless, the trend is toward cloud computing and you may not have a choice before long. Like it or not, I believe this is where the market is moving.

Chapter 6: Cost of the Cloud

Now that you have a good understanding of cloud computing and how it works, let's take a look at some of the economics that you should be thinking about as a nonprofit.

The first is a shift from capital expense to operational expense. This is much harder for nonprofits than it is for for-profits. Many of us who run nonprofits are accustomed to writing grants. And capital grants are generally easier to obtain than operating grants. So, when it comes to buying a new server or new computers, we often look to our donors who write checks for capital grant requests. The only issue with this is it is usually not proactive. Our tech guy or gal tells us that the server is starting to fail or the drives are full or the server is out of warranty. Only then do we start thinking about writing a grant for a replacement. It takes time to write a grant and usually longer for it to be approved. This can leave the organization worrying about the failing server or dipping into reserves with the hope the grant will come through later. Either way, it is an uncomfortable solution. Wouldn't you rather be focusing on delivering your mission than worrying about the failing server in your back closet?

Having spoken with several large grant-making organizations, I can tell you that they really do not like making grants for technology. They understand it as a necessary evil, but would rather allocate their resources on a program or toward building capacity. There is little social return in a new server or five new laptops. And, let's face it, most grant-writing organizations have the same issues we have. They need to report on how they spend their money and what social return they gain on their investments.

On the other hand, cloud computing relies on services. If you remember the characteristics of cloud computing, then you know that it is metered. You only pay for what you use. But that usage is generally measured monthly. So if you are using an email system that costs $10 per user per month, you will need to calculate the number of users you have using the system to know what your costs will be for the month. These are operational costs. What is good about them is they are predictable. You can plan for these costs in advance. And remember, they scale. So, if you are planning to add a new employee in the second quarter, you know that they will also need an email account, and you can increase your budget $10 a month to account for the new person's email. This makes planning for technology easier. It may also help you focus your grant-writing on more meaningful requests. A new van to transport your clients, a new medical device for animal intake, or extending the size of the greenhouse to grow more food are much more exciting grants to write, and to extend, than new servers and laptops.

I suggest conducting a cost analysis on any technology purchase. If you are thinking of getting a new server, include all the costs associated with that server. It is not just the cost of the new piece of equipment, although that is significant.

How much is it going to cost you to configure the server? How much is it going to cost to transfer your data from the old server to the new one? How much energy does the server use in a month? How much will you need to pay for maintenance? Are you extending the warranty? Could you use the floor space that it takes up for something else? If so, how much is that floor space per square foot costing you? What other costs do you have? Are there any soft costs like employee time to manage the machine or the vendor? Make sure you add them all up when comparing an on premise solution to a cloud solution. I do not think that the on premise servers will go away for some time, but I do think smaller organizations should think about getting out of the business of purchasing, managing, and maintaining

Small to medium sized nonprofit organizations spend between 2.5% and 5.1%, on average, for non-salary related expenses.

servers. It is just not a core competency for most nonprofit organizations, and it is not adding value to the organization. Even as an IT company, I offload as much of the technology to the cloud as possible. It is just a better solution for a 25-person company.

The National Technology Association, or NTEN, recently published a report on nonprofit technology staffing and investments. This is largely compiled data from a survey they conducted. In the report, they define small nonprofits as having an operating budget of less than one million dollars. Medium nonprofits are defined as having budgets between one and five million dollars. Everything in this book is meant to address these organizations. Larger organizations have more complex needs and different considerations. They probably also have resources to think through and plan for some of these issues. Regardless, the survey revealed some interesting information about budgets. It found that most organizations that have budgets between one and five million dollars do not have a full-time IT person, especially those on the lower end of that range, and spend between 2.5% and 5.1%, on average, for non-salary related expenses. The survey also found that the level of technology adoption does not necessarily correlate to the organization's budget. This means that even though organizations are spending a larger percentage of their budgets on technology, they may not be leveraging the latest tools or have the best infrastructure to support their organizations. In fact, the study notes that many organizations in the five percent spending range characterize themselves as "struggling with technology."

A long time ago in my career, I learned about the cost of quality and spent a great deal of time and effort learning the quality manufacturing principles. One of the most counterintuitive principles I learned was that quality can improve at the same time cost is decreasing. You *could* have both. Who would not want that equation in business? I had a very hard time believing that you could decrease cost and improve quality until I saw it in action. Costs decreased because quality improved. Now that I am older—a lot older—and wiser, I understand these principles. Oil changes are a good example of this principle. I used to change my oil for about $30 every 3,000 miles. Now I change my oil every 10,000 miles and spend $70. This is because of synthetic motor oil. Overall, the quality of oil improved, and the cost of oil decreased by about 30%. I also get back some time because I am getting at least two fewer oil changes for every

10,000 miles of driving. Of course, there is a positive impact on the environment as well. These are exactly the principles I look for in computing.

Computing, and cloud computing in particular, has experienced these same types of advancements. I have found that we are able to significantly lower our computing costs, while increasing the quality. This is especially true because we are a nonprofit. There are many companies willing to donate some services—even software as a service—to nonprofit organizations. So, a service, like email, for instance, that used to cost our organization a significant amount of money to run, we now get for virtually no cost. And, it is better—more reliable, more feature-rich, more stable. That is a really big advantage for us. We have found that by making some small investments up front to migrate to a new platform has paid big dividends on the back end.

> **For a medium sized organization, this can mean up to $30,000 in annual cost savings. That is significant. That is like getting a new donor—a big one.**

We no longer have a server to maintain for our email—or replace, for that matter. We no longer need to go through the process of upgrading our software. We no longer need to troubleshoot it when the system is down. And, we are guaranteed that our email will be available to us 99.9% of the time. All this costs our organization nothing. I will explain later how we do that and what opportunities are out there for nonprofits, but this is one heck of a value proposition.

Some of my calculations suggest that for small to mid-sized nonprofits, technology spending can be reduced while improving their quality of computing. I believe for most organizations, the cost can be driven to the 1-2% range. For an organization that is spending 5% on technology, this translates into a 60% reduction in cost. Also, it almost always translates into improved quality of technology; if these organizations have better technology, they can serve more people. If they can reduce technology costs, they can put that savings toward their programs. For a medium-sized organization, this can mean up to $30,000 in annual cost savings. That is significant. It's like getting a new donor—a big one. That is probably enough to hire part-time program staff or deliver more services.

There are also soft costs. The younger generations have a totally different experience with technology than baby boomers. They grew up with technology. They know how to use it and they expect it to work. When it doesn't, they become frustrated; therefore, productivity costs need to be factored in as well. You will have a hard time attracting and retaining younger employees if they cannot access their email or other applications they need to do their job. (And by the way, they are probably going to want to access applications on their iPads and their smartphones, too.) Instead of fighting this, think about how you can make these employees more productive. It will reduce your costs. You will get more program delivery if your technology works well.

Of course every organization is different, but I challenge you to take a good look at what you are spending on technology today and see if there are some opportunities to reduce your costs and improve your computing systems. Take a long-term view. If you are spending $10,000 today, what is the five-year return to the organization? I bet it could be significant. That is a much more compelling grant to write to a funder than a server replacement job. They will be excited to help you make your organization more efficient, especially if you can translate the cost savings into more program delivery.

Part II – The Tools of the Trade

Chapter 7: Virtual Servers & Desktops

Now that you have a basic understanding of cloud computing, let's dig into some of the tools that are available in the market. Virtual Servers and Desktops fall under the category of Infrastructure as a Service (IaaS). They are not specific applications for a business need, but it is underlying architecture that supports these business applications.

Virtual Servers

Let's start with virtual servers. Early in Chapter 2, I described what makes the cloud the cloud and the underlying principles of virtualization. Virtualization software, as you may recall, will allow you to parse a physical server into numerous virtual servers. Virtual Servers have whatever amount of physical resources that you allocate to them, provided that the actual physical server has that many resources to provide. So, a server that has 16 GB of memory and a hard drive that has 500 GB could be broken into four virtual servers with 4 GB of memory and 125 GB of storage. This enables me to set up a virtual server and allocate only the amount of computing resources I need to run my applications.

Many companies have started to provide these virtual servers as a service. You can go online and purchase these resources. It is like renting a server that is delivered as a service. Take a look at Microsoft Azure, RackSpace, or Hosting.com. All of these companies will allow you to rent a server. You tell the company how many resources you need on that server and what operating system it should run. You then load your applications on that server and run the applications from their servers in the cloud. This is especially popular for organizations that need to test an application, are developing an application, or would like to analyze a large amount of data very quickly. They can spin up a server in minutes instead of hours. This service can also be used by small to mid-sized nonprofits. We have clients running their applications on cloud servers. The reason for this is they may have migrated most of their services to Software as a Service in the cloud. But they may have that one application that was not ready to move yet. In that case, a cloud server is a good alternative to purchasing a new physical server.

Cloud servers, however, are a temporary solution. Most small business software will be delivered as a service. If that becomes true, eventually there will be no need for a nonprofit to have a virtual server. The virtual servers all will be managed and maintained by the companies that are providing the software services.

Virtual Desktops

Virtual Desktops are similar technology. Most of use a desktop computer every day. We need to be able to draft a document, respond to an email, or forecast our budget on a spreadsheet. All of the resources that are required to perform those functions are usually delivered up right from your local computer. The computer has an operating system and runs the productivity software (word processing, spread sheeting, etc.), and you can save documents and data to your internal hard drive. A virtual desktop, on the other hand, delivers all of these services without using your local computer. Some companies refer to this a Desktop as a Service (DaaS). The desktop lives in the cloud. Since you now understand cloud computing, you realize that that the desktop is on a server in a data center. The way that virtual desktops work is that they are delivered over the internet and you access them by going online. Once you navigate to your online desktop, they will often look the same as what you are accustomed to seeing on your computer. The most common operating system is Windows. So maybe what you are presented with is a Windows 7 desktop. Your applications can be loaded on that operating system, so you may have a full Microsoft Office suite presented on that desktop. If your virtual desktop has persistent storage, then you will be able to save documents, your family photos, and other applications to your desktop.

What is the advantage to having your desktop in the cloud? Well, there can be several advantages. First, since the device is not relying on local computing power, you can use a less powerful computer. You are accessing your desktop over the internet, so you only need a browser and a good internet connection. Forget that your machine is 10 years old and falling apart. If it breaks down entirely, you will not lose any of your data, or even your operating system, because nothing is stored locally. This means that nonprofits can finally accept those donated computers and genuinely say thank you. If you are running desktops as a service, the donated machines will work just as well for getting to the internet as a newer machine. This can provide significant cost savings to the organization.

Maintenance on a virtual desktop is also better. Let's say your employee navigates to a website and a pop up comes up suggesting that they have a virus and they need to run a scan on their computer. This is often how malware (malicious software) is introduced. If you have ever had a computer virus, and I suspect most of you have, you know how troublesome they can be. They can grind your computer to a halt and keep you from being productive for a day or more while a tech works on the machine to get rid of the virus or reload the operating system and applications. With a virtual

---

Many small businesses are spending between $35-$100 (and more) to maintain their desktops and laptops.

---

desktop, the image of the operating system is stored independently of the data, so a technician can simply delete the desktop image, give you a new one, and attach your stored data. You will be back up and running in minutes without ever noticing a change.

At this point, you are probably wondering why anyone would not want to use a Desktop as a Service or a Virtual Desktop.

Well, they can be expensive to run. As I write this, the market is about $50 per desktop per month. That is almost the cost of a new laptop for one year, so it can be cost prohibitive. However, if you are paying an internal resource or an outsourced provider to maintain your desktops, then you need to factor that cost as well. We recently conducted our own research and found that many small businesses are spending between $35-$100 monthly (and more) to maintain their desktops and laptops. Since maintenance is included in the cost of a virtual desktop, that makes $50 start to look a lot more attractive. Back out the cost of maintenance, even at $30, and now you are paying $20 for Desktop as a Service. That is a lot less expensive for really good technology. That easily pays for itself over three years because you will not need to buy machines. And if you do need to add computers, you could buy one for $200-$300 and not a $700-$1,000 laptop.

Of course, if you are running all of your software in the cloud as a service, you really do not need much computing power. A virtual desktop could be overkill. You may be able to get away with simply using an old computer because all of your software can be accessed over the internet and uses no local computer resources to perform all of the functions you need. Or you can purchase those $200 netbooks and get to everything you need. Hopefully this is really starting to articulate the power of cloud computing.

This is where it pays to really think through what your organization needs. If you are a distributed organization with offices around the country, or even around the city, and you have the need for hosted applications because they are not available as a service, then virtual servers and virtual desktops are worth exploring. One of the areas I see this the most is for organizations that have invested in using Blackbaud products like Financial Edge or Raiser's Edge, which are very heavy applications and are not offered yet in a true software as a service model. They will require being hosted on either a local server in your office or a virtual server in the cloud. That will not hold true for long. I am sure these companies are developing their software to be delivered as a service, or they risk becoming irrelevant. But, until all applications are delivered as a service, there will be a need for virtual desktops and virtual servers in the nonprofit sector.

Chapter 8: VoIP

We have not talked a lot about telecommunications, but it is worth a chapter. Just as data can be transmitted over the internet from a data center to your office, voice can also be transmitted over the internet. I will not get into the underlying technology, but voice can be broken down into data and sent over the internet. This is what enables VoIP or Voice over Internet Protocol. This can be a great tool for a nonprofit organization.

With VoIP, your phone lines can be delivered as a service. They can be hosted at a provider. I have seen a lot of pricing on VoIP, and most of it is between $20 and $40 a phone per month. I have often found organizations that are paying two times that for phone service. The great thing about VoIP is that it is delivered over the internet, and most of the systems are networked in a way that is very intelligent. Let's say you need to move offices. You can now take your phone system with you to your new office. Your phone number, and extension, follow you.

Take a look at your phone bill. It is could be one of those services you just pay every month and do not think much about. See how much you are spending; this could be really low hanging fruit. When I talk to clients about improving quality and reducing cost, this is often the first place I look. Many of us have been sold phone systems or phone contracts over the years. The phone providers are notorious for designing long-term contracts that are hard to break, but

I simply open my email and click on the file. I can instantly listen to the message on my smart phone, PC, or tablet. That is efficiency.

there is always a point when you can get out of the contract. Know when your contract ends; it could be your opportunity to bring in better service at a lower cost.

Internet-based phones are loaded with features. My favorite is something called Unified Communications. When someone calls my office (which is a VoIP phone) and I am not available, they are routed to my voicemail. There is nothing special there until they leave a message. When they do, an email is created and automatically sent to me. Contained in the email is the voice message. I simply open my email and click on the file. I can instantly listen to the message on my smart phone, PC, or tablet. That is efficiency. There are many other features, as well. Auto attendant is another great one. Instead of having a receptionist answer incoming calls, there is an automated feature that allows the caller to select the extension, or look up the person in a directory, or get routed to a particular department. This is a very professional way to manage incoming calls. You may no longer need a receptionist. Perhaps that is another area of cost savings.

Every VoIP system has its own features and benefits, and they are usually related to cost. What I prefer is hosted VoIP. Much like a hosted application, a VoIP phone system can also be hosted. This means a service provider is responsible for all of the technology in the background, and the server is required to manage the voice and data traffic. The only piece of equipment in the office is usually a switch and router. Those are very easy to install and maintain, and usually your provider will manage that equipment for you.

When your system is hosted, you have some more flexibility in how you use your phone. The service my office uses allows me to take the phone home or on the road with me. I can unplug the phone in my office and plug it back in at home. The network will know that my phone has relocated and will route any incoming calls to the phone's new location. This is great for a flexible workforce. I have team members who live hundreds of miles from the office. They can easily work from home and have full use of their office phone. A customer will never know the difference; the phone rings normally and the caller ID shows the call being placed from our office. You can even transfer the call to a coworker across the country, as if he or she were right next door. If you have a remote workforce, the cloud can really enable great technology solutions for your organization.

There are more features, like forwarding calls to your cell phone when you are out of the office, and even call center technology. Like most services, there are plenty of providers and differences in pricing and features. You will want to shop around to find the best offer. Most will not include the phone equipment, and if they do, the price will likely be higher. But that can be a good use of a capital grant because the phones are likely to be useful long after they have been depreciated. And, that means a lower monthly cost for a basic service.

Keep in mind that you will still need an internet connection. In our office, we are able to run all of our voice and data over one connection. The larger the organization, the more bandwidth you will want to consider for this increased traffic. We sometimes find that the phone system has been sold alongside an internet connection. In many cases, we also find that organizations have been sold what is called a T1 line. These are dedicated connection lines and they certainly have their place. But now that most internet service providers' (ISPs) costs have decreased, they offer much more bandwidth than a T1 connection does for a fraction of the cost. When we install VoIP systems, we often end up working with our clients to replace their ISP, which can result in thousands of dollars saved and much faster service.

If you are in a long-term phone contract, mark your calendar with a reminder about 90 days before it expires. Chances are, you will need to give your provider some notice that you want to end the contract and you will need some time to shop for a new vendor. If possible, stay away from long-term contracts. Anything over 36 months is really too long. And I would only consider a 36 month contract if I were amortizing the cost of any new phones or hardware in the contract. The service costs will undoubtedly decrease over time.

Chapter 9: Data protection

Another service that is important to understand is your data backup. I have written about the various types of Infrastructure as a Service offering, but one that is more discrete is data backup and recovery services. Whether you use cloud computing or not, it is important to back up your data. I have worked with many nonprofits over the years that have experienced a server crash in their offices.

It happens; servers fail and disk drives fail. Just about anything that has a moving part has a lifecycle. For disc drives on most servers, that lifecycle will be between three to five years. Other things can also go wrong, like floods, fire, and contamination. These are less likely, but still possible. It is important not to worry about all of the possible things that can happen to corrupt your data; just be sure you have a good backup system in place and a plan for business continuity.

Many organizations are sold servers with what is called a RAID (Redundant Array of Inexpensive Disks) configuration. This means that there are several hard drives that make up the server. If you hear the term RAID 5 that means there are five different hard drives in the server. Their job is to take pieces of the data and spread it around onto different drives so that the data is not all stored in one place. If one of the drives fails, or more likely *when* a drive fails, the data will have been on several drives and replicated. This allows the server to recover the data for the missing drive. This is not a backup plan. I have seen servers in organizations that have had three out of five drives fail without anyone realizing that even one had failed. This can cripple an organization. It can cost thousands of dollars to try to recover data from a failed drive, and often the data is unrecoverable.

Your data is part of your lifeblood. Imagine not being able to access your email, saved files, donor management data, accounting data, and client information. Try explaining to your board that your organization is at a standstill because you lost a hard drive or three. That is not a meeting I want to attend, especially when it may cost the nonprofit a significant amount to attempt recover the data on the corrupt drive.

> **Try explaining to your board that your organization is at a standstill because you lost a hard drive...That is not a meeting I want to attend. Especially when it may cost the organization a significant amount to attempt recover the data on the corrupt drive.**

There are several ways to manage your data. One is to have a USB drive plugged into the back of the server. I have seen many nonprofits do this. The plan usually is to have two of these drives; you can obtain a significant amount of storage for a relatively small price and swap them weekly. That way, if something happens to the onsite data, like a fire, you will have most of your data offsite, at least up until the current week's data. The major flaw with this is that most organizations do not have the discipline to swap the drives weekly. Someone goes on vacation or someone forgets, and the next thing you know, the data that is offsite is not a week old, but a month or more. That can be a real issue if you experience a data loss. Imagine trying to recreate a month's worth of data. I usually advise against a USB drive swap plan.

There is the other extreme: cloud back up. I have worked with organizations that like all of their data backed up to the cloud. Since that is off their site, it does provide a much better protection strategy. But this can be very costly. Cloud storage is probably the most expensive. It depends on how much data you are storing. If you are a small organization, you may be able to get away with a service that backs up all of your data for $25 a month or so. A larger organization may have more data and the costs can add up quickly. It is good to know what your data looks like and how much you have. I have seen some pretty big hard drives that are full of employees' pictures and music files. You really do not want to be paying to store your program manager's iTunes files.

If saving money is important, you may consider a hybrid approach to data management. Some organizations purchase a Network Attached Storage device, or NAS for short. This is an appliance, like a USB drive, that attaches to your server. Data is then stored on that device, which likely has at least two hard drives. So, there are now at least two copies. You can then decide which files on that device have the most important data and back up those files offsite to a cloud storage provider. If your accounting files and donor files are really important to your organization, you may want to also back up those files to an offsite location. This reduces the amount of data that you are storing offsite and thereby reduces the cost. This can be a really effective solution. The NAS devices are usually around $500 or so for a significant amount of data. Cloud storage is expensive, but you do not need as much.

This is a good case for cloud computing. The more you can offload to a Software as a Service provider, the less data you will need to maintain. For instance, if your donor management system is a cloud-based solution, your solution provider will be backing up and storing your data. You will want to make sure they maintain more than one copy of that data in a second geographic location.

No matter what option you select for your data management and protection, just make sure you select one and that you understand the risks and benefits of your selection. You will want to test recovering whatever solution you are using. That will enable you to understand what the recovery process is like and what timelines are reasonable for business continuity. For instance, if your server fails and you need to obtain a new server, it can still take a week or more to get back online. Imagine that you still need to purchase a new server, load the operating system and applications, and then transfer the saved data onto the server. If you are operating a cloud server, that process can be cut to a day or less. And if you are using SaaS based solutions, you should not ever lose your data and you should be back up in a matter of minutes or hours, not days.

If you take away only one piece of advice from this book, it is to find a strong solution for backing up your data.

Chapter 10: Emerging Cloud Services

This is going to change rapidly. Like all technology, it moves at a lightning fast pace. But, I have noticed a few things in the way of cloud services that are emerging.

The first is Single Sign On. Several companies have created a service that allows a company to manage their user's profiles and passwords. A few companies in this space are Okta and Simplify. They can integrate with your active directory, which is where user profiles are stored and accessed to authenticate the user, or as a standalone authentication service. I really like these products; they help to create a better end user experience. Since there is only one password to remember, and all the apps are in the same place, it makes for an efficient workspace for employees. This tool allows the administrator to demand strong passwords from the users and since they only need to remember one it can be more complex. It also enables a Bring Your Own Device culture. If you have workers who want to bring their own computers, tablets, and smartphones to the office and access your data, this kind of a tool is helpful.

In a Single Sign On (SSO) environment, the administrator maintains the applications and assigns applications to the users. These can be set up as profiles. If you have an accountant profile, for instance, that would have the usual applications that all employees have, but it may also include access to the accounting and payroll systems. Your marketing profile, on the other hand, may have access to Twitter, Pinterest, and other applications that are more applicable to his or her position. What I love about this is that it makes it easy to add someone to the organization and remove someone else. In either case, it is very helpful. Everyone wants the new employee to feel welcomed and hit the ground running on day one; this helps an organization prepare and manage user profiles. And, if you have lost an employee who harbors negative feelings about the company, the last thing you want is him or her walking off with your Twitter password. Single Sign On provides a way to instantly shut down a user account.

Another emerging area is analytics. More and more, we are able to gather data analytics as a service. This is particularly true in social media. If you want to know how many users are reached with your tweets, there is a cloud-based service for that. There is also a service that tells you how much influence your tweets have in the social media world. And, of course, there are web analytics that tell you how much traffic is coming to your website, where they are coming from, and what they are looking at while they are there. This area will only continue to grow as social media continues to become more important.

Finally, I see a lot of apps being developed. This is not necessarily new, but the way we are using them is changing. Instead of big applications that manage an entire business process, which can be very expensive, more discrete apps are emerging that manage only one piece of a process. That allows an application to solve 80% of the issue with a business process and break away from the need for custom programming. Instead of a HR system, you can purchase an application that allows you to track employees' time off, or an app that allows you to give performance appraisals. These are generally "plug-and-play" and very easy to learn. They are also mostly delivered as a Software Service, which means you do not need to store the data. As large platforms like Salesforce.com and Microsoft Office 365 dominate market share, they will continue to grow an ecosystem of apps. Instead of trying to solve all the problems themselves, they are opening their platforms to the development community. The developers can then create small applications that reside on the platform and provide value. It is much more of a free market system, which means there is competition that drives the best apps for the lowest price. This is a big advantage for the consumer or business that needs those applications.

The cloud is here to stay, at least for the foreseeable future. We are only at the beginning of the innovation and adoption cycle for many of these services.

Part III: Leveraging the Cloud for Nonprofits

Chapter 11: Collaboration and Productivity Software

As nonprofits, we have some advantages. Many foundations, corporations, and individuals admire and respect our work. In addition to donations and volunteer hours, some companies offer services that provide value to the sector. And in many cases, those services are offered pro-bono, or are completely donated. Fortunately, there are some technology companies that make their products and services available to the nonprofit sector. One of these services is e-mail.

There are two major players worth noting; the first is Google, whose highly publicized Gmail is free. While the email system works well, it is not terribly feature-rich. I usually recommend hosting and managing an Exchange service over using Gmail. In my opinion, Gmail is not an enterprise class system. I grew up using Microsoft products and am more comfortable using their systems. I simply find them more intuitive and more integrated with Microsoft's other software products. That said, Gmail is free and for very small nonprofits, it is adequate. One of its strengths is that it is helpful for a distributed workforce since it is a completely hosted cloud-based system. Google also offers Google Docs, a free office productivity software package that includes spreadsheet, word processing, and presentation applications. It allows users to create a presentation or document and then share it with other users (who must have a Google account.). Again, it is a nice service for free but it is far from enterprise class.

> **Fortunately, there are some technology companies that make their products and services available to the nonprofit sector.**

Microsoft is the other large provider of these services. Typically, their service has been offered through donated software for Exchange and Office licenses. TechSoup, a nonprofit based in San Francisco, has worked closely with Microsoft and other software providers to help distribute highly discounted and donated software products. Microsoft Exchange and Office have been the staples of their program.

In the last couple of years, Microsoft introduced a new service that was initially named Business Productivity Online Suite, or BPOS. That has evolved to what is now called Office 365. This is service that is on the Microsoft cloud and includes email, collaboration services, and productivity software. The email works in conjunction with Microsoft Outlook, with which most end users are familiar, or as a web-only service on a platform named Outlook Web Access. The interfaces and features are similar to Microsoft products. In fact, many users will not even notice a transition from an on-premise hosted Exchange server to Office 365. The software looks and behaves the same way. This is a big advantage in terms of user adoption. It also works seamlessly with their productivity suite, which includes Microsoft Word, Excel, and PowerPoint.

The Lync software is also included. If you are not familiar with Lync, it is collaboration software that is rather intuitive. You can use it to see which of your colleagues are available and send them instant messages. But you can also use it to collaborate on documents together and share your screen with them. It is very powerful and part of a future office concept. Imagine you and your colleagues are part of a distributed team and are working on opposite coasts. Your software will tell you at what time you are both available and then you can instant message one another to review a project you may be working on together. You can then make changes to your document or presentation in real time. That is pretty powerful.

I absolutely love Office 365. I jumped at the chance to move our office onto the platform. It provided us with the ability to decommission our Exchange server, which required a great deal of time, effort, and money to support. The Office 365 platform is very intuitive and easily accessible from any device including tablets and smartphones. And, I never have to worry about losing our data. Like any service, it does go down, but it is rare, and it comes back up very quickly. Microsoft guarantees a 99.9% uptime on the product and that is exactly what we have experienced. It is often one of the first recommendations I make to our customers.

As part of Office 365, SharePoint, a document management and collaboration system, is included. This is another easy place to get immediate benefit. SharePoint has allowed our group to move all of our shared files to the Microsoft cloud.

More than that, it has allowed us to take that messy drive with hundreds of folders and organize them in a logical manner that aligns with how we run our business. For instance, we took a look at the high level functions we perform—our services, programs, human resources and finance, development and fundraising, and board management. We then created folders for each of those high level categories. From there, we added documents that everyone could find. A powerful search feature is also included. What I love about this is the security. I can give permission to all employees to view the human resources handbook, and block access to sensitive employee salary information to everyone but a select few. On the board management side, I can store documents like minutes, board presentations, and corporate documents, and provide access to our board members. I can decide if they can simply view the documents or if they also have authority to make changes. I think you are probably starting to get the picture.

One powerful feature, and I eluded to this with the board example, is that I can provide access to my SharePoint site to people outside our organization. This means the board of directors can access the board site on SharePoint without us requiring any additional licensing. Of course, if you work with partners to provide your services, a feature like this can be very productive for collaborating. There are whole books written about the features and functions available as part of SharePoint; suffice it to say that it is a very powerful tool included in certain licensing packages of Office 365.

In addition to SharePoint, Office 365 includes something called SkyDrive. Think of SkyDrive as your computer's hard drive or your personal folder on the shared drive. It is a place where I can store all of my documents that are not going to be shared. They are in the cloud and backed up, and I can access them from anywhere—even my mobile phone. This enables me to keep some documents private and not rely on my local computer for storage. It also gives me built-in data protection for those files. I now keep nothing on my local desktop. If my PC were to crash, I could easily buy another one and be up and running immediately simply by navigating to Office 365. There I would find my email, shared files, personal files, and important company documents.

Over the last year, my organization worked with Microsoft to provide donated licenses of Office 365 to charities. By the time this is released, that program will have been formalized and most nonprofits will be eligible for these services as a donation. That is a game changer that provides instant savings to an organization and better software. There are many Fortune 500 companies and government entities that run on this platform and are more than willing to pay for it because the service is really valuable. That it will be donated to many nonprofits is remarkable. We can run our businesses like many large companies and save our dollars for our programs. That is incredibly generous of Microsoft and very valuable for the sector.

> **We can run our businesses like many large companies and save our dollars for our programs. That is incredibly generous of Microsoft and very valuable for the sector.**

If you are a small nonprofit, with an operating budget under $5 million or so, I would suggest looking at this platform. You can immediately eliminate the server in your back office, or significantly free up space on the servers you are maintaining. Even freeing up space has a significant impact. Larger organizations should consider doing the same; the economies of scale will be even greater.

The costs associated with purchasing and maintaining a new Exchange server, as well as the cost of purchasing the software, are all eliminated in this model. Microsoft is making a significant impact on the sector by providing this service at no cost to nonprofits. They are not just donating the software, but also the services. They still need to have servers running in their data center and people to maintain those servers and software, and that is also donated. In my opinion, this is the most generous contribution they can make.

Chapter 12: Databases

Almost every nonprofit organization uses a database. Many use multiple databases. Of course, there are some that do not use them, but probably should. We use databases for managing our donors' information, volunteer information, and program information. We could not live without them. Some databases are simple, like Microsoft Access. Others are much larger and more powerful, like Oracle. Some are developed and highly customized for specific tasks, like donor management. There are probably at least 50, and maybe 100 or more, choices for donor management databases on the market. If you are shopping for a new database, I would suggest you check out Idealware (www.idealware.org), a nonprofit that evaluates and develops reports specifically focused on nonprofit sector software. Many of their reports are free or very inexpensive.

Traditionally databases have been installed on a local server. Of course, with cloud computing, that is all changing, and most databases are available in the Software as a Service model. This significantly speeds up time to market for many nonprofit organizations. Deploying a server and installing a database once took days or weeks; now you can deploy a database in a matter of minutes. If you are using a database that is on your server, check with the company that supplied that database. Chances are, they now offer a cloud-based version, or they soon will. I believe most nonprofits will not use server-based databases in just a few short years.

One of the most powerful software as a service databases I have used is Salesforce.com. Don't let the name fool you. This database was initially developed as a CRM or Customer Relationship Management software. It is used by many Fortune 500 companies to track sales opportunities and customers. They use it because it is easy to deploy, requires no maintenance, and the data can be accessed from anywhere at any time. This is particularly important for companies with a distributed team or a mobile sales team. In the nonprofit sector, we play on the words *Customer Relationship Management* and talk about the database in terms of a *Constituent Relationship Management* system.

What you will find is that many of the processes of managing a sale or a customer are very similar to managing donors, volunteers, and clients. It is about relationships. What do we know about our donors? They have a name, address, phone number, and email address, just like a potential customer. We want to know their history. What is the last donation they made? Did they attend our gala? What is their lifetime giving history? Have we ever asked them to consider increasing their donation? Now consider that you have this information, and much more, on every one of your donors. You can now run reports that tell you how many donations you have received this year or this month. You can find out how many tickets you have sold to the gala. If these are reports that you use often, you can even have them automatically generated and emailed to you with whatever frequency you desire.

There are also dashboards, which provide metrics that I may want to monitor. I can elect to have a dashboard of various measures sent to me by email each morning so that it is the first thing I see in my inbox. That is powerful. And by the way, the functions and features I just mentioned require no coding. The report builder is very intuitive and it is relatively easy to create new reports that I need. I can also elect to share them with the team or keep them private. Databases can be segmented. I may have an area that keeps track of my donors and another section that tracks volunteers. I can give all employees access to everything, or restrict access. But all of my data is in one place that is safe, secure, and easily accessible.

Salesforce.com is only one of a number of databases on the market. Microsoft has an incredibly powerful and flexible database called Dynamics. That has the same capabilities as the Salesforce.com system. It often comes down to dollars and cents when making a choice. Both companies are generous with their technology. The Salesforce.com foundation manages donated licenses to charities and offer up to 10 donated licenses per organization. These are their enterprise licenses, which are their most powerful licenses, which normally retail for about $1,500 per user per year. So think of that as a $15,000 donation. However, any licenses over 10 will require a fee. They do discount the additional licenses at 80%, which is more than reasonable, but the costs can still add up for a larger organization. Microsoft has a different model. They highly discount their software as a service offering of Dynamics to $10 per user, per month. That is incredibly inexpensive, and if you have a large team of employees that require access, it can be less expensive to have $10 Microsoft licenses vs. 10 free Salesforce.com licenses or a number of others that cost $300 per user, per year.

These are the 800 pound gorillas in the market for nonprofits. They come as a blank slate and require some configuration to process the management of clients or constituents. You will want to customize them. You will want to label the fields to reflect your processes and nomenclature, and you will want to develop your own reports. There are some accelerator packages for each system that are very nonprofit friendly, but you will still want some customization. This is where these systems can get expensive. The skill set needed to manage a project like this is considerable and expensive, but it may be worth it. If I can pay to have it built and then have very low ongoing costs for the system, it is probably worth doing.

> **These are very powerful pieces of software that not long ago only would have been used by larger corporations because they were too expensive for most nonprofit organizations.**

Most of the other databases on the market, especially Software as a Service applications, have implementation costs and ongoing monthly or annual fees. However, for very small nonprofits that do not have extensive requirements, there are some lightweight systems that may serve 80 percent of the functionality you need for a lower price point. This is why I point you to Idealware's report on databases. It is extensive and gives you a lot to think about. I realize it is not very exciting to consider all of these things, but it is a significant investment and an important part of running the business. You may also decide to work with a consultant to document your requirements and scan the landscape of systems that would be appropriate for your organization.

No matter what database you select, I would strongly consider having it delivered as a service over the internet; otherwise it will require more maintenance and probably a server. Ask whichever company you are planning to use about the various delivery models they may have and what their plans are for having the application hosted on the cloud. There has been, and continues to be, a lot of consolidation in this market, which makes it a bit risky; however, as long as you have access to the data, you should be able to map it and import it to another database in the future if the company ceases to exist. Make sure that there are provisions for that in whichever company you hire for your database services.

The databases that I mentioned, Salesforce.com and Microsoft Dynamics, are available to most nonprofits at the discounted or no-cost options. These are very powerful pieces of software that not long ago only would have been used by larger corporations because they were too expensive for most nonprofit organizations. As nonprofit leaders we have an excellent opportunity to take advantage of these powerful databases to increase the effectiveness of our organizations.

Chapter 13: Back Office and Custom Software

The other staple in most small business software suites is an accounting package. Like databases, there are a lot of choices. These systems are also being built and delivered in a Software as a Service model. One of the first cloud-based software services I ever used was our accounting system.

For nonprofits, there is a lot of choice and some good news. Many software companies will also donate or highly discount their accounting software to nonprofits. I will highlight a couple.

The first is QuickBooks. Nonprofits are eligible for nonprofit discounted QuickBooks software and it is easily obtained by going to TechSoup. They have various packages to offer, including some different versions of their client server-based licenses. But they also now offer QuickBooks online for an ongoing monthly fee. I understand that some of the features and functions of the online version may be lacking what is offered in the client server-based package. I am sure that they are working hard to port that functionality into their online version, as they realize that is their future revenue stream.

Another popular package is NetSuite, a powerful and entirely online software program. Not only does it handle all of the bookkeeping and accounting functions, but it also doubles as a Customer Relationship Management (CRM) system. What I love about NetSuite is that it is cloud-based. I can view my accounting reports on the fly and with the latest updates from any machine at any time. That is incredibly helpful for running a business.

If you are 100% in a cloud based environment, you will have greater flexibility, greater reliability.

Along with accounting software, there are many other related systems that are being delivered over the internet. These include payroll systems like ADP and Paychex, online HR systems, and banking systems. The trend is absolutely toward online systems to run back office operations.

I am not prescriptive in what applications you should use to run your business; everyone has his or her own preferences. But I would not be investing in a package these days, as a small- to medium-sized nonprofit, if it were not delivered over the web.

It is best to involve all of your constituents when making changes to your system. I would never make a decision to change accounting software packages without consulting my accountant and testing the system to make sure it meets our business requirements.

There are also many specialty and custom packages on the market. Some handle very specific functions like program measurement, program reporting, and vendor management. These can be stumbling blocks to moving to the cloud. Many applications were built to manage a very specific task for one organization. These have often been built in an older technology and are struggling to stay relevant. Because the preferred architecture at the time was client server, many of them rely on server-based technology. These will hold back organizations from fully adopting cloud computing. This is where a hosted server or a hosted desktop can be very relevant. They can be stepping stones to a 100% cloud environment. Small applications like QuickBooks can easily be hosted on an image as small as a desktop. Something larger may require a virtual server. In either case, if the only thing holding you back from a full cloud-based environment is one older custom application, then it is worth investigating your options.

Remember, if you are 100% in a cloud-based environment, you will have greater flexibility, greater reliability, and some of the other benefits that were outlined in chapter five, like the ability to fully outfit your organization with thin client computers and eliminate your servers altogether.

The best advice I can give is to take a comprehensive view of what is on your server and what can be eliminated. Go through the exercise of finding out what it will cost to move completely to a Software as a Service model and see what benefits, tangible and intangible, your organization can achieve.

Chapter 14: How to get started

In this book, I have outlined what the cloud is, how it works, and some of the features of cloud-based applications. The big question is: Where do you start?

Anytime you are going from one place to another, a map is helpful. If you want to embrace the new technology, you will need a plan. Start by developing a list of all the applications that are on your server. You will also want to develop a list of all applications that you are running over the internet. Collectively, these will be everything that runs your business. This will tell you where you are today.

Now, start to allocate costs to each of these items. The internet-based software should be easy enough. The server-based software will be a bit more in depth. You will need to take into account the cost of the server, the service to set up and maintain a server, and any software purchases you are making. Of course, there is still more to consider. You will want to note what you are spending on your computers and as well as any maintenance they require, and what you are paying in your backup solution, antivirus solution, and so forth. Try to develop a very clear picture of your technology environment and what it is costing you.

After you have taken the time to go through this exercise, some things will become apparent to you. You will see some of the opportunities to reduce costs or improve your quality of service. Others will require more research and discussions with a vendor, or several vendors, to see what solutions are available.

The long term goal you should be exploring with your service provider or support team is how to increase ease of use, decrease cost, and improve quality. I advocate for developing an easy-to-use platform. It helps with employee adoption and reduces costly maintenance expenses. Idealware has some tools for technology planning and their fees are relatively inexpensive, but you have to have the discipline to do it yourself. The other option is hiring a firm or consultant to take you through the process; this is slightly more expensive but may be worth the investment if you are overburdened with other pressing items in the business.

You will also want to spend time educating yourself about what options are on the market and available to nonprofits. TechSoup is a great place to start for some of that research, as they have software and services available to nonprofits. I would also suggest talking with your board members. Many of them can be great resources for technology or may have access to resources in their companies that could help you build a roadmap.

Once you have your starting place, your journey will be more evident. Start by developing a matrix of some of the items on your list. Break them into four quadrants: high cost savings and easy to get done; low cost savings and easy to get done; high cost and hard to get done; and low business cost savings and hard to get done. You will see immediately where you can focus your time. Pick off some of the low hanging fruit in the high cost savings and easy to get done quadrant. Think about developing a plan for the high cost savings things that require more work. Table the items that are hard to get done and do not return much value.

This is a great way to be proactive about your technology environment. Eventually, you may not have a choice about how you purchase and use your software solutions. You may have experienced that already with some of your decisions on technology. The sooner you embrace a plan, the faster you will get to an environment that does not require a lot of support and is easier for your employees to use. It will be more predictable in terms of cost.

Most of what I have discussed are about providing a stable and secure platform for your computing needs. My hope is that you will get your organization to a place where everything works and works well. Then you can focus your technology thinking time differently. You can consider what new applications will make a difference in delivering services. Is there a push notification tool that you can use to communicate with your constituents more effectively? Can you develop an app about your services in Spanish so that you reach a greater number of people? Can you

I often hear that technology is a real albatross for many nonprofit executives. They did not get into their jobs because of technology. Most may have a distaste for technology because it can be such a burden. So the best thing is to make it simple, stable, and inexpensive. All of those can be achieved through cloud computing.

develop a measurement system that is meaningful to your organization? There are many possibilities. Organizations are using technology to deliver more services, reach more people, and do more good.

Cloud computing is not magic; it is just a different way of managing many of the same tasks. It can be more efficient, especially for small to mid-sized organizations. It does not solve all of your problems, but it can bring efficiencies. Much more important is to develop the plan, or roadmap, on how to improve your overall computing platform for the long term. Many nonprofits have the ability to drive computing down to a very simplified level that is stable and secure. That platform can also be very predictable in terms of cost and scalability. I often hear that technology is an albatross for many nonprofit executives, and that is understandable; they did not get into their jobs because of technology, and many have a distaste for it because of the burden it places on them. The best thing is to make technology simple, stable, and inexpensive. This can be achieved through cloud computing.

Either way, for the immediate future, cloud computing appears to be here to stay. It benefits the software vendors and end users alike. Over the next few years, the cloud may become so pervasive that we will stop calling it the cloud – it will simply be the way computing is performed. As I stated in the foreword, my hope is that in the future, you do not think about computing for computing sake or for how to get your work done; it just works and works well and is no longer a source of frustration. At that point, you can start to think of how your own app may be developed to serve more of your constituents. You can use technology to deliver more services. You can use technology to make the world a better place.

www.ingramcontent.com/pod-product-compliance
Lightning Source LLC
Chambersburg PA
CBHW022113170526
45157CB00004B/1614